1960s Racing Car

Viking Longship

Locomotive

Spy Plane

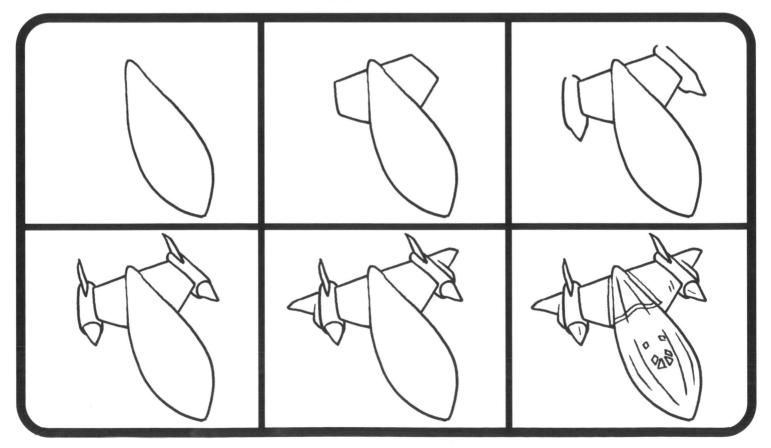

Formula 1 Racing car

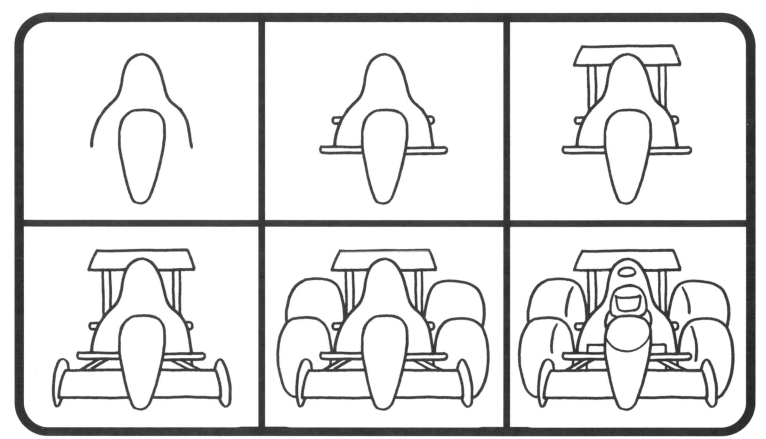

Roadroller

Cruise Ship

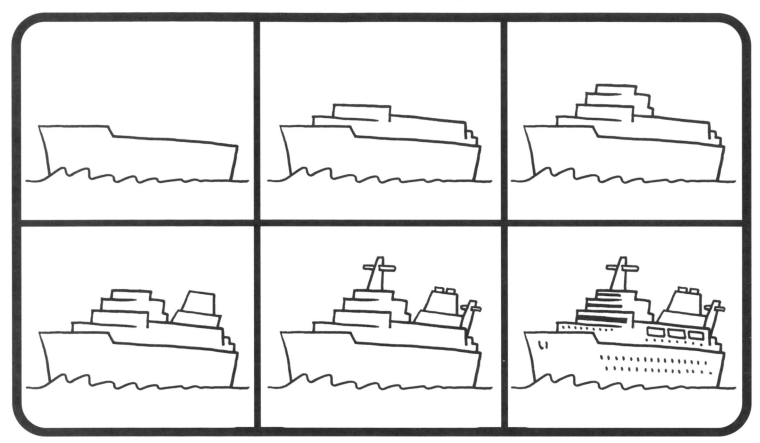

Chopper Bike

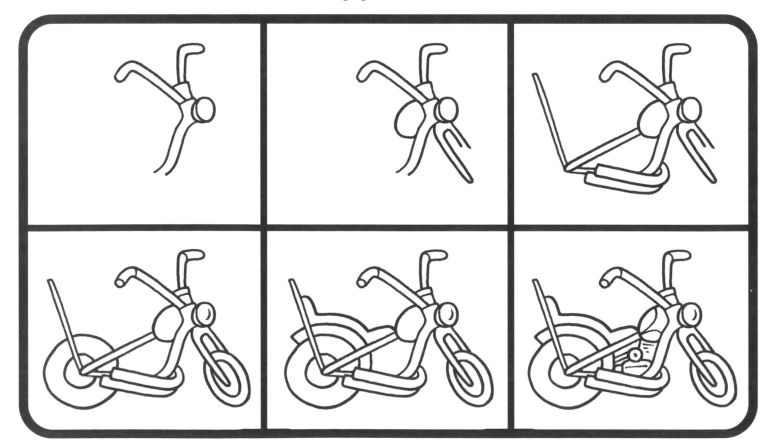

747 Jumbo Jet

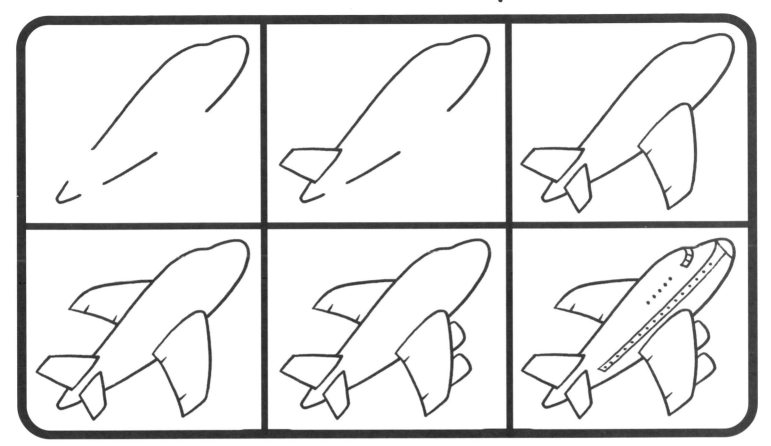

Custom Car

Micro car

Digger

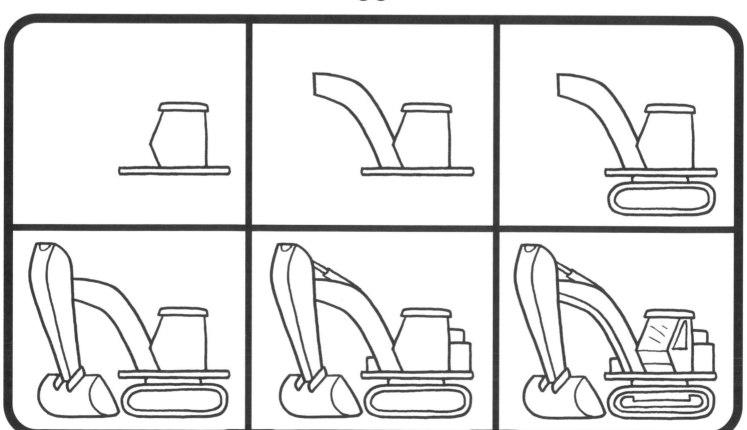

Lifeboat

Helicopter

Ski-bob

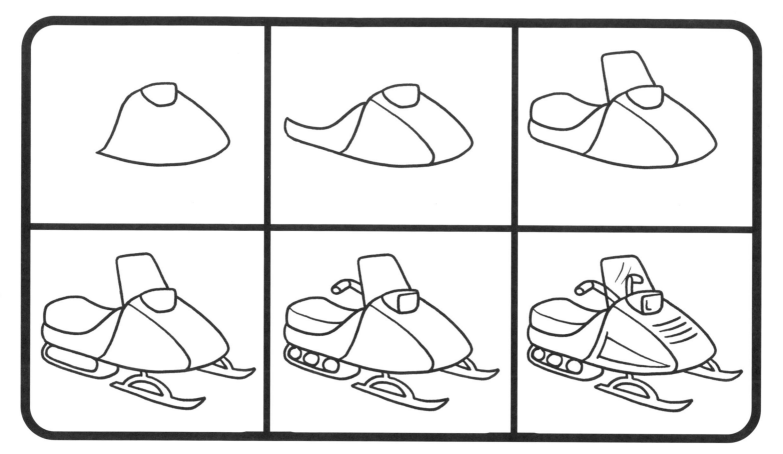

Moon Buggy

Crane

High-Speed Locomotive

combine Harvester

Racing Motorcycle

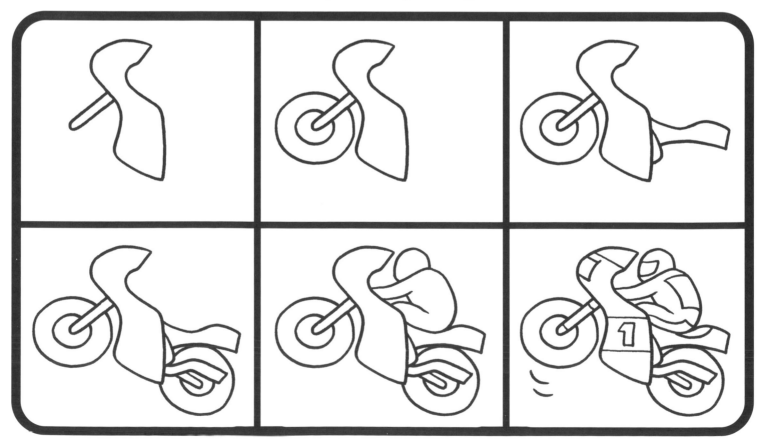

Police car

Wright Brothers' Flyer

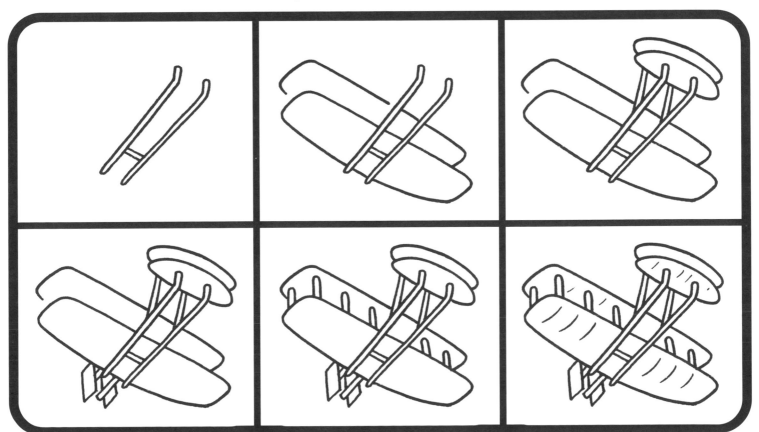

Mini Digger

Jet Ski

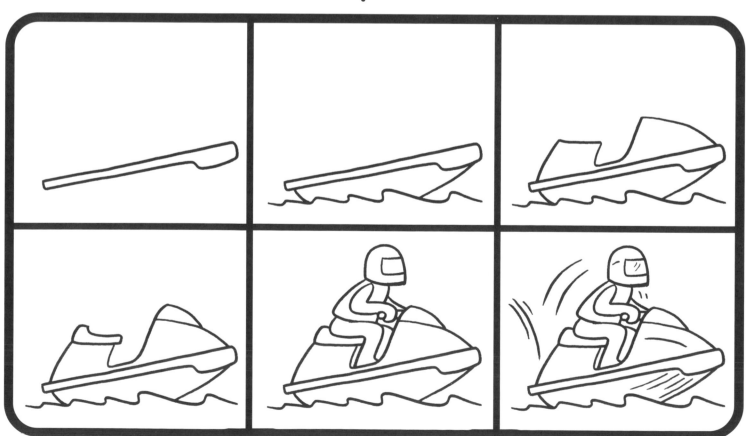

Space Shuttle

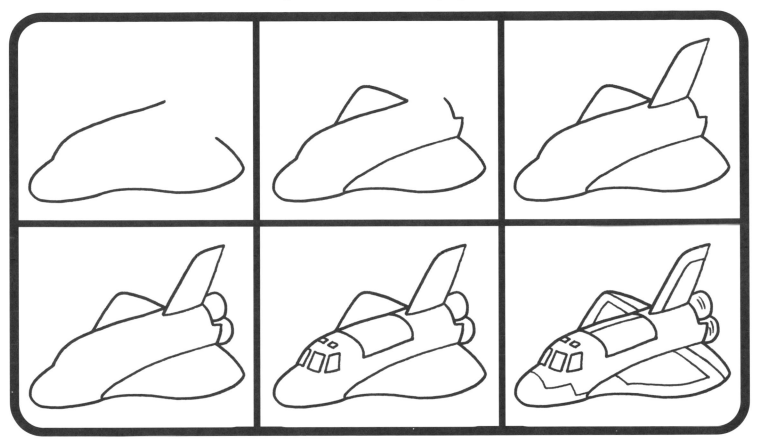

Chinese Junk

off-roader

Bullet Train

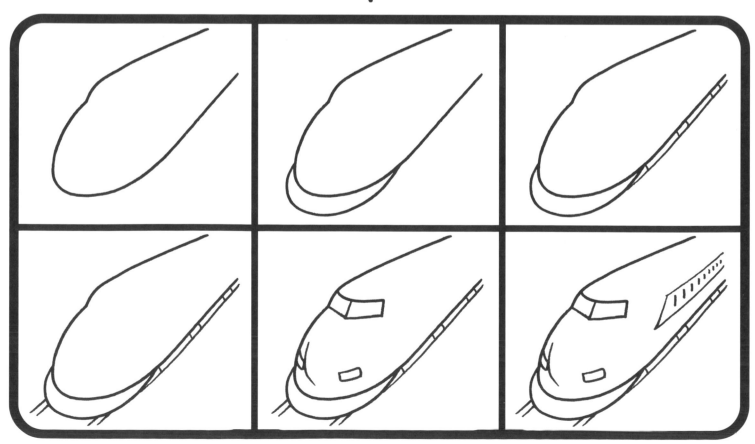

Motocross Bike

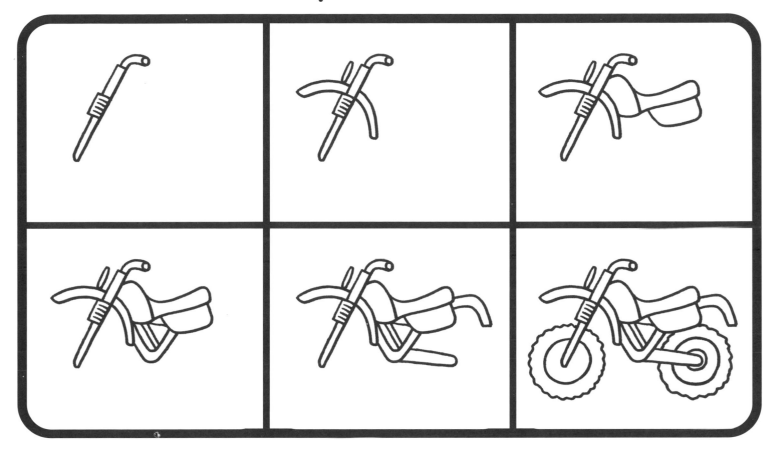

Traction Engine

Stealth Bomber

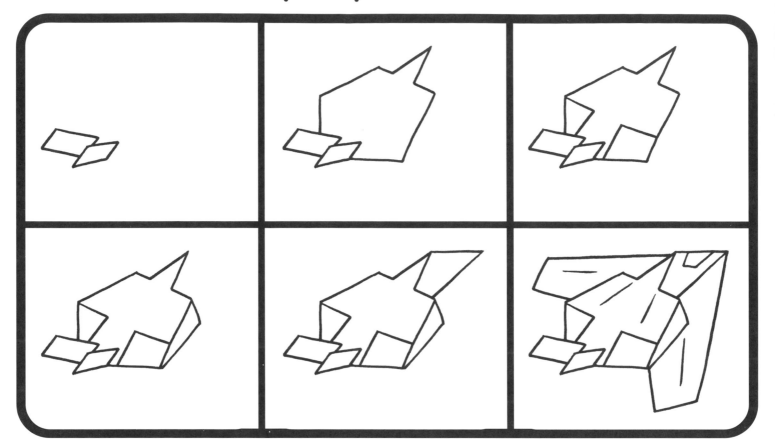

Early car

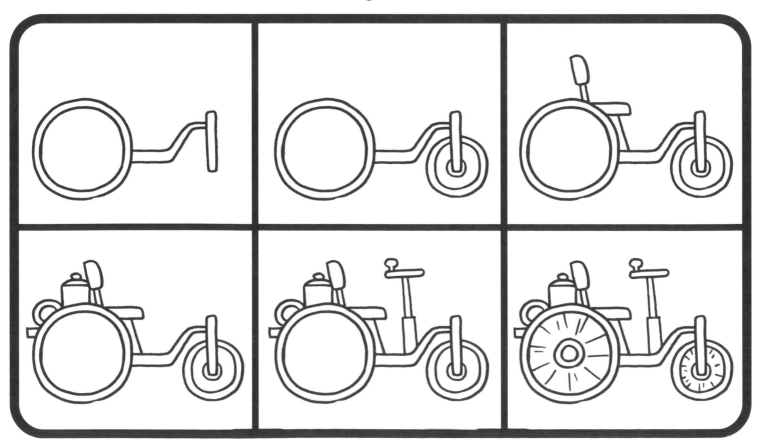

Tipper

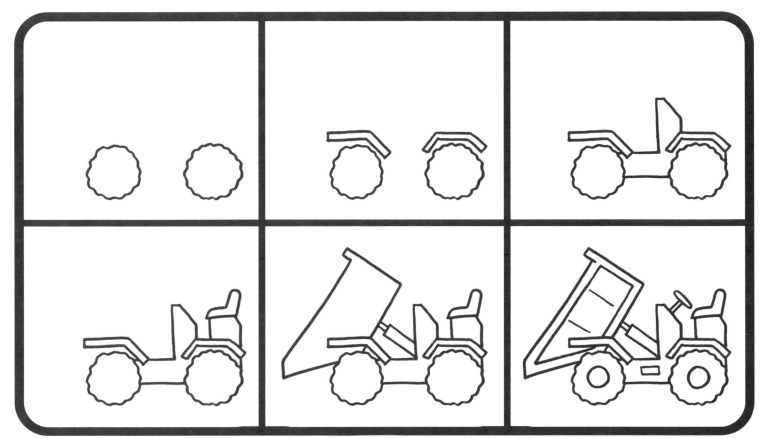

Cadillac

Motorized Ricksha

Hydrofoil

Snowplow

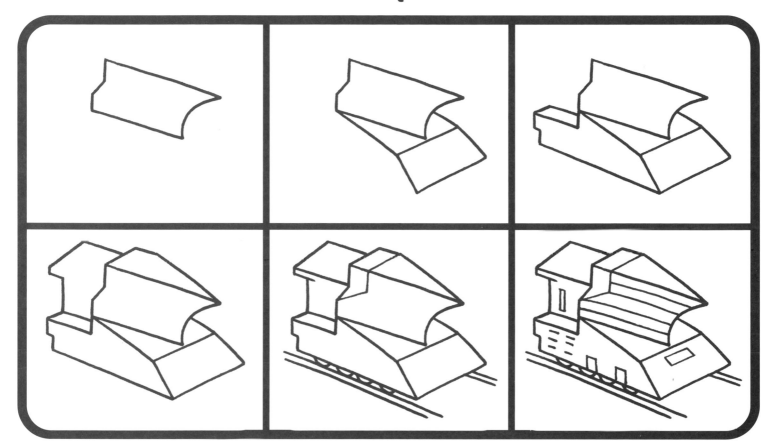

Spitfire

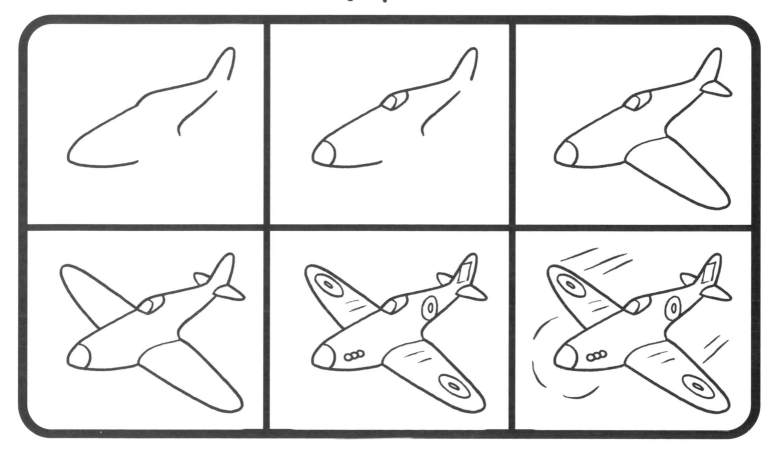

Bubble Car

Cement Truck

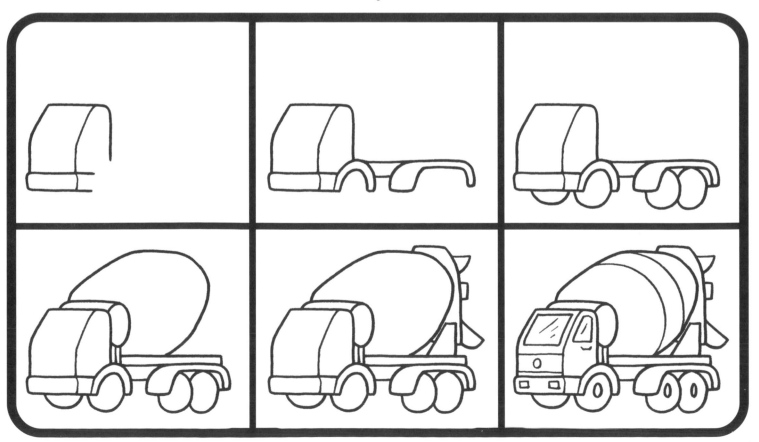

Ultralight

Paddle Steamer

17th-Century Ship

Monster Truck

Dumper Truck

Scooter

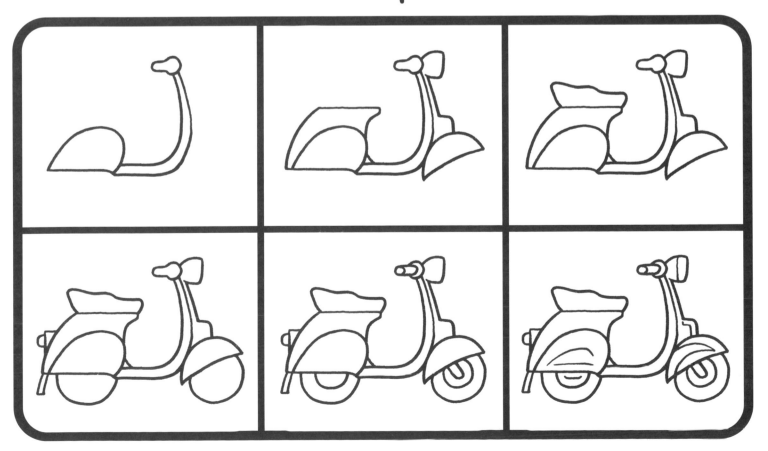

Le Mans Racing car

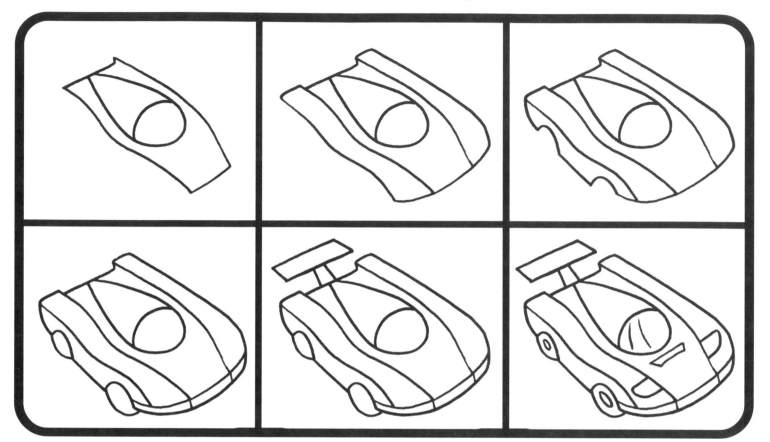

Dumpster Truck

Hovercraft

The Mallard Steam Locomotive

Roller

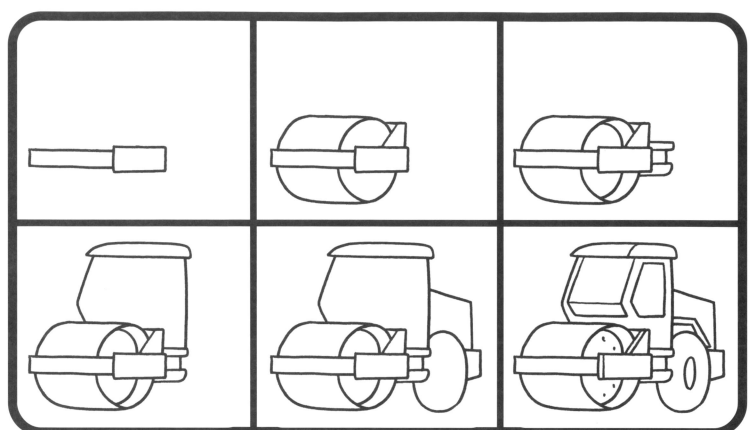

Fishing Boat

Pick-up Truck

Truck

Speedboat

1901 oldsmobile

Seaplane

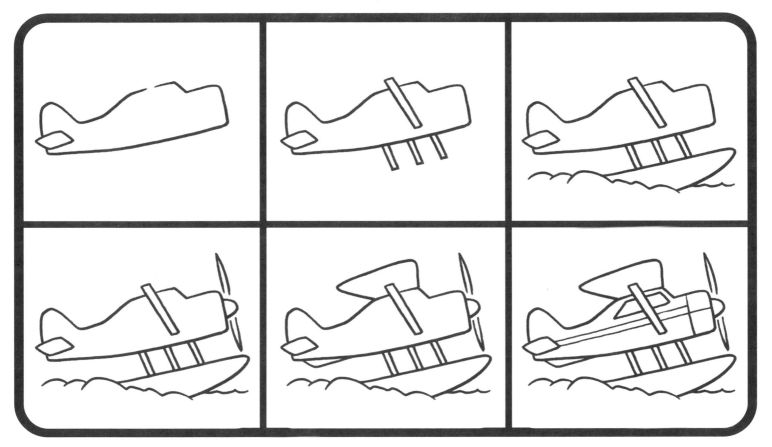

London Bus

Tractor

Snowcat

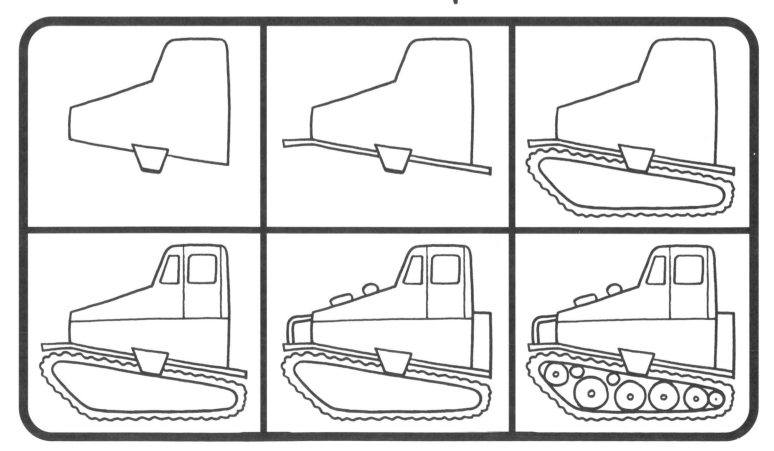

Fire Engine

Stock car

Supersonic car

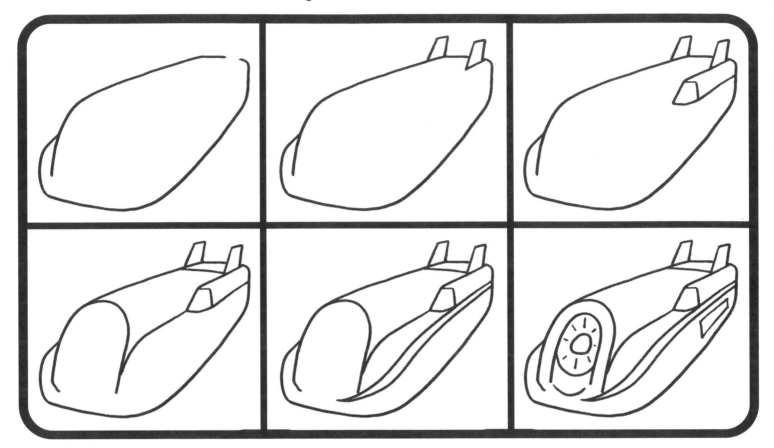

Tugboat

Stephenson's Rocket

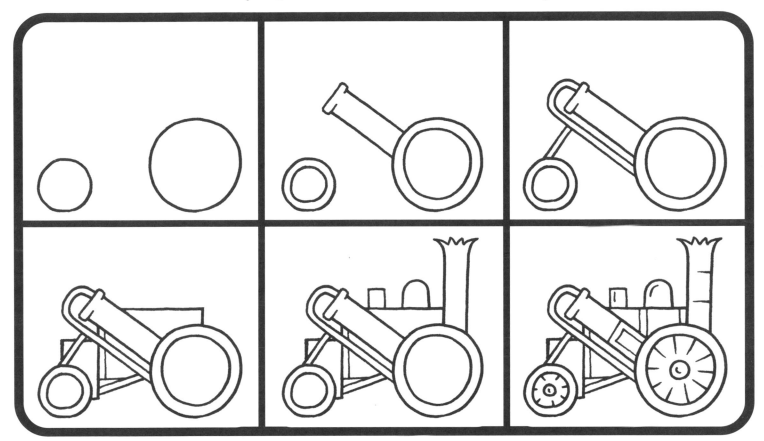

Small car

Quad Bike

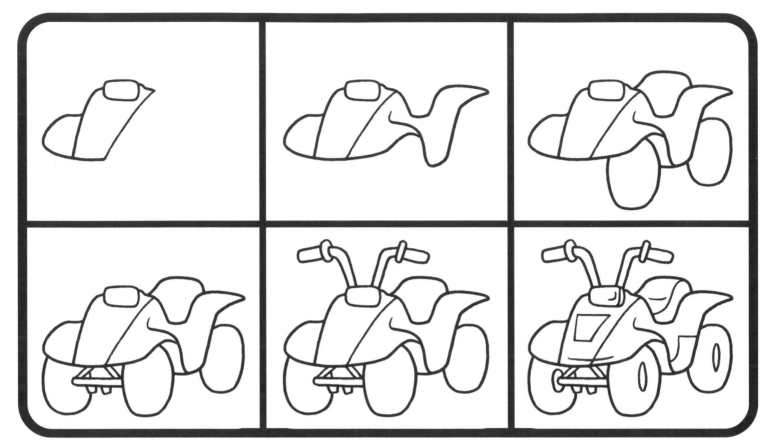

London Taxi

Bus

Submersible

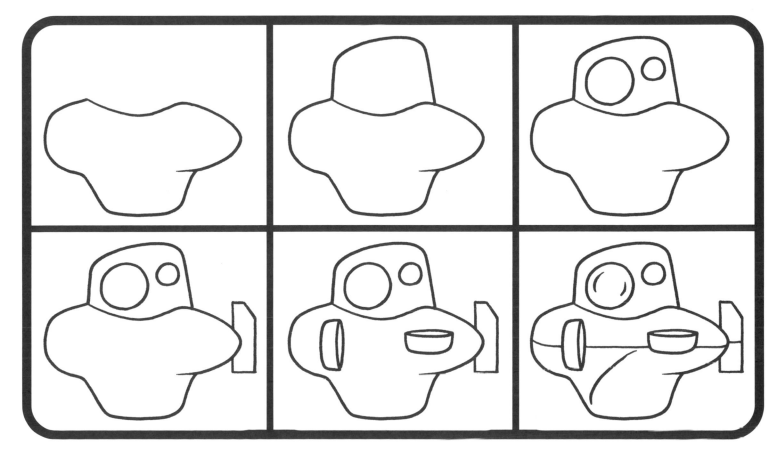

1920s Motorbike

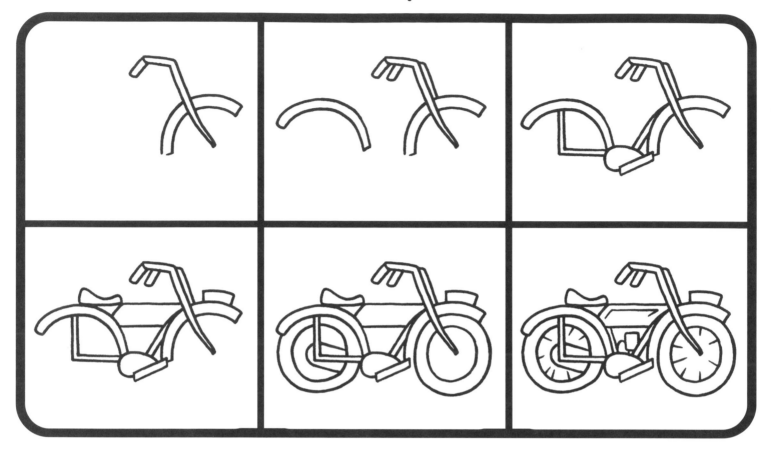

Concept Electric Car

Bulldozer

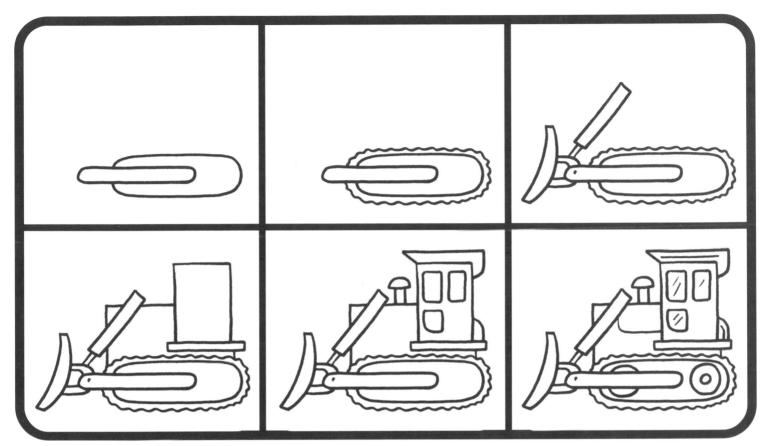

Sport Utility Vehicle

Rolls Royce

Light Aircraft

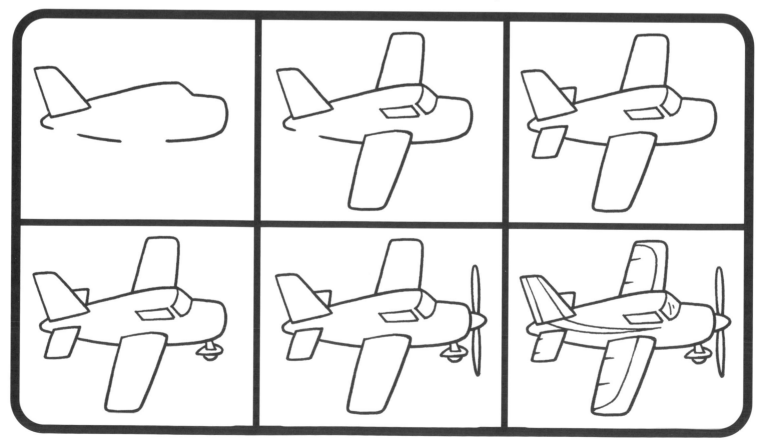

Dragster

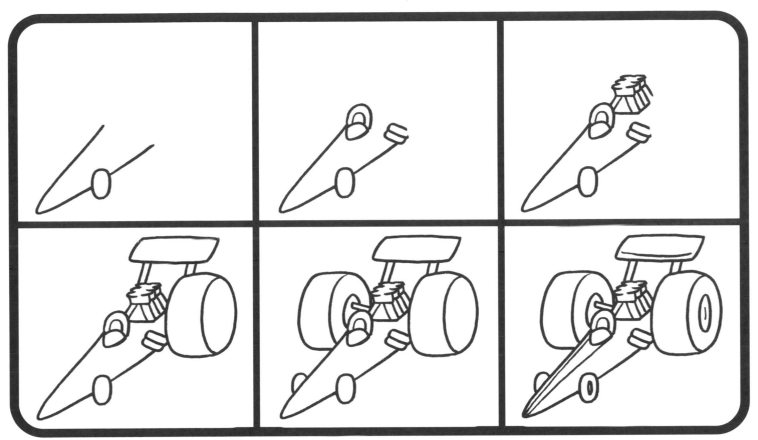

Wild West Steam Locomotive

Model T ford

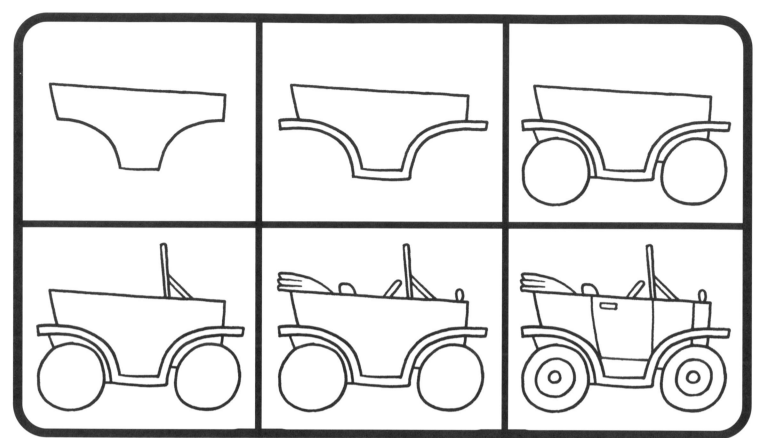

Dune Buggy

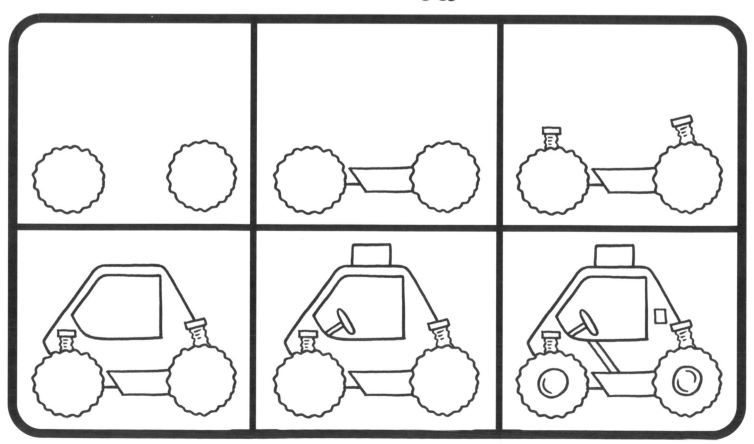

Gossamer Albatross

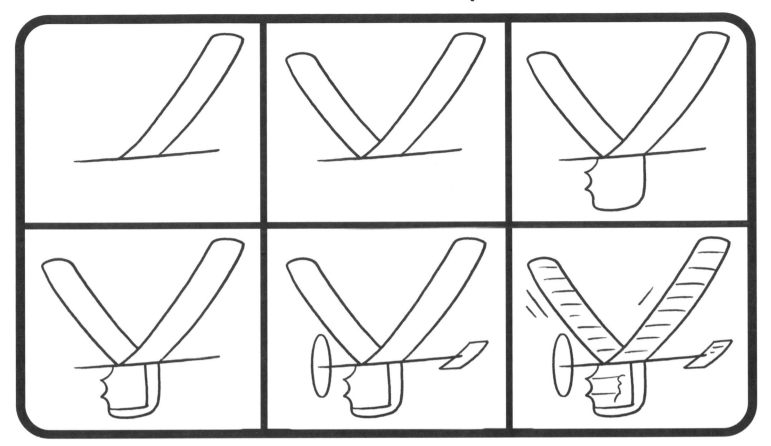

Forklift

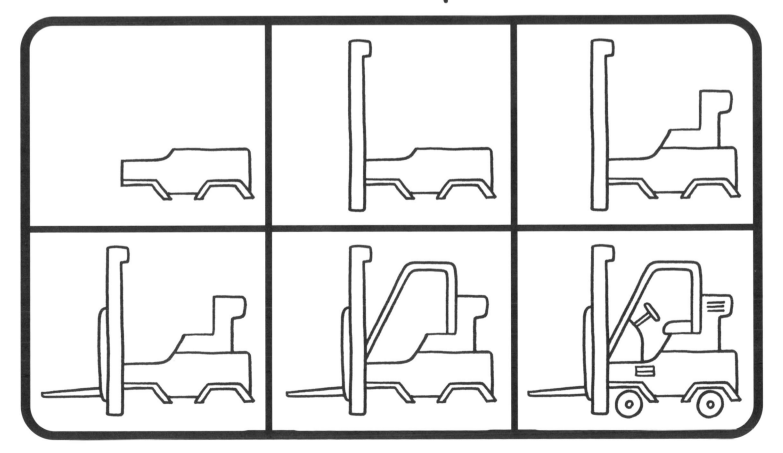

concorde

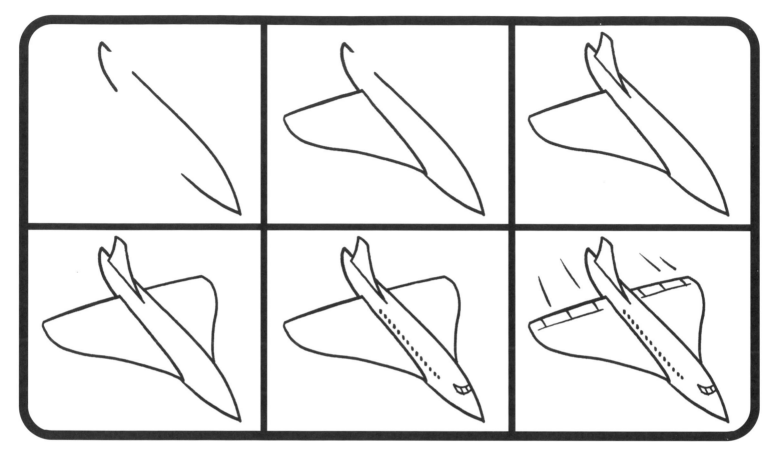

Stretch Limo

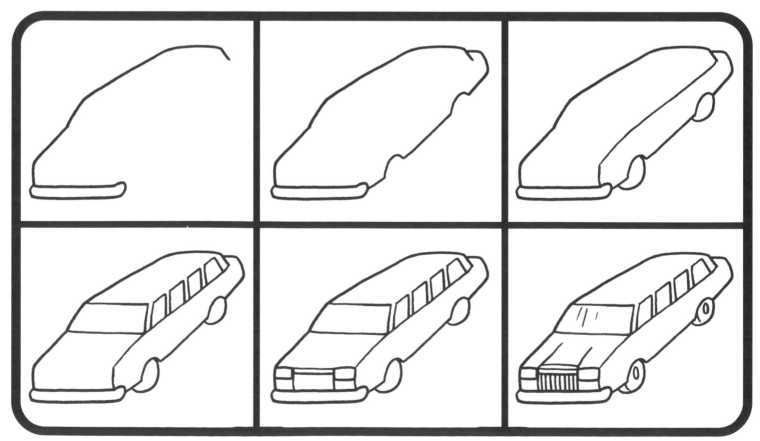

Yacht

Jeep

Submarine

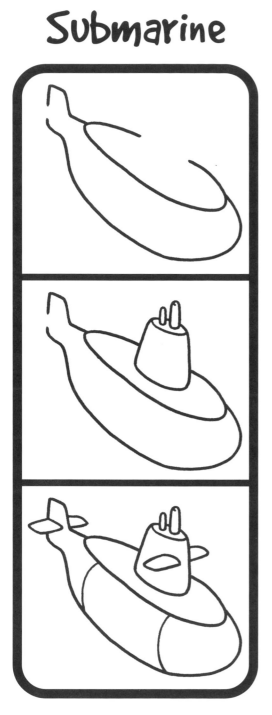

Bi-Plane

Monorail Train

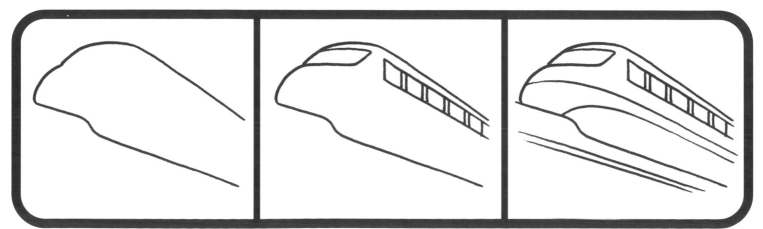

cable car

Sunray

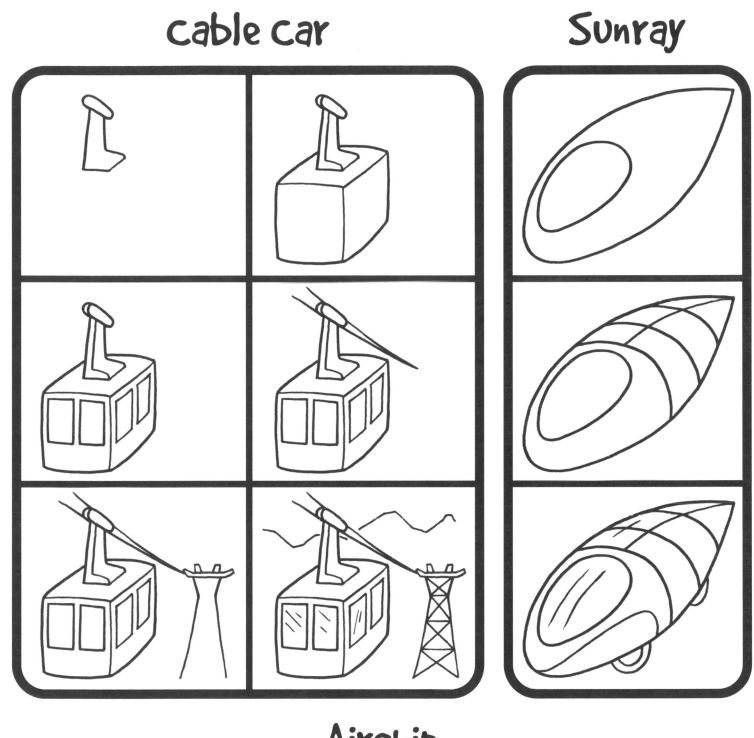

Airship

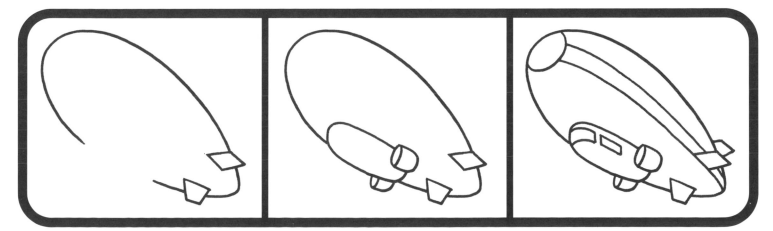

VW Beetle

Van

Hang Glider

funicular

Rocket

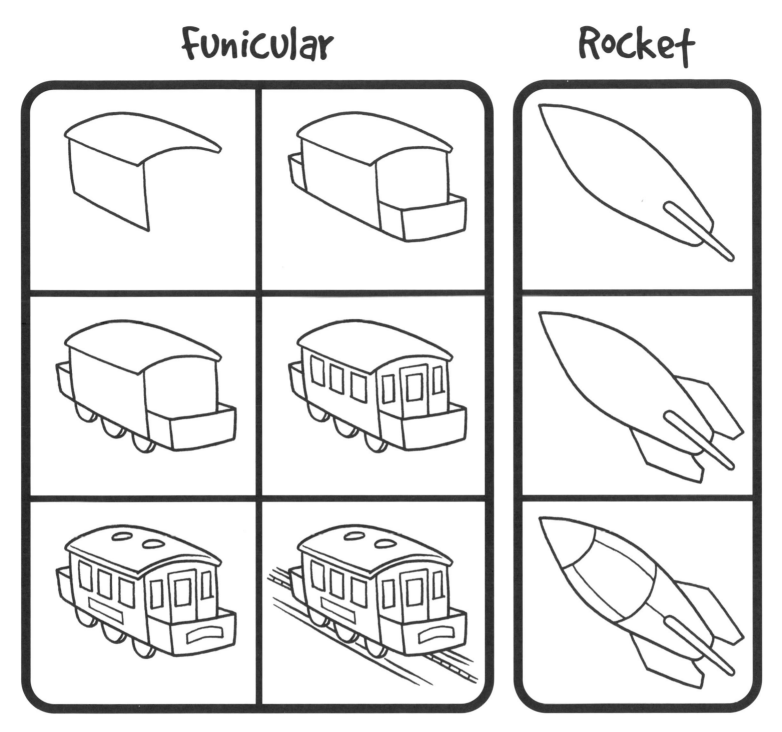

Lindbergh's Spirit of St Louis

Glider

Trolley car

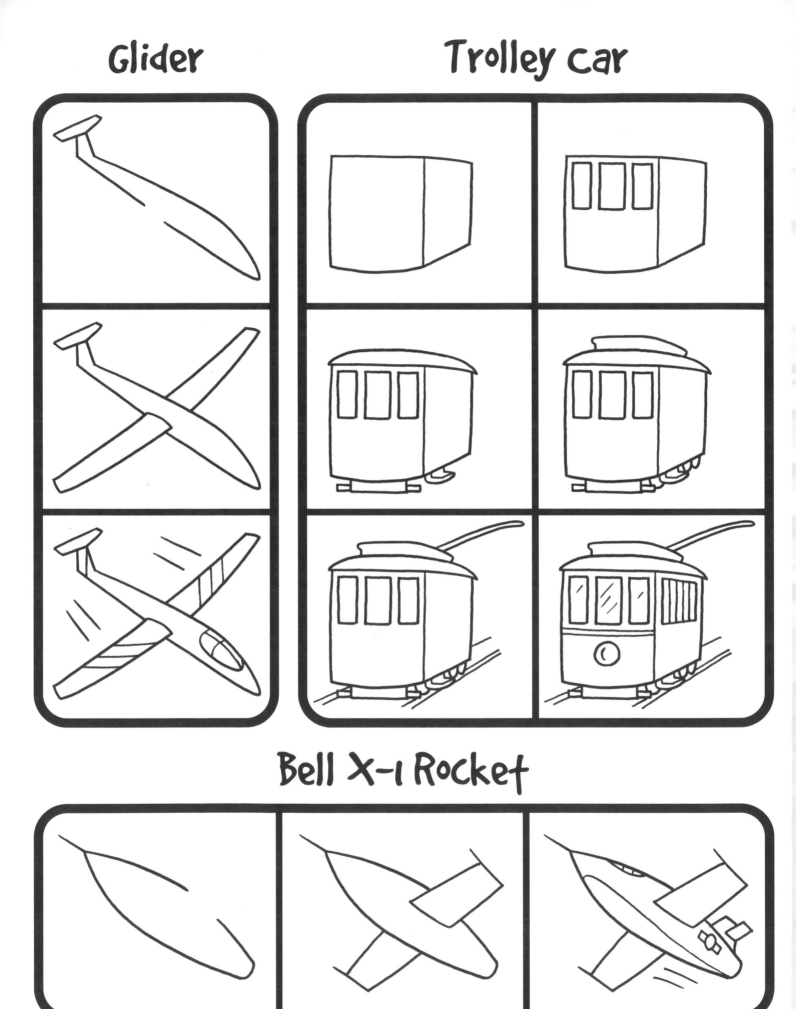

Bell X-1 Rocket